GREEN TIGER'S
ILLUSTRATED
A·B·C

GREEN TIGER PRESS   MMV

GREEN TIGER PRESS • A DIVISION OF LAUGHING ELEPHANT BOOKS • 3645 INTERLAKE AVENUE NORTH 98103
FIRST PRINTING • ALL RIGHTS RESERVED • PRINTED IN SINGAPORE
WWW.LAUGHINGELEPHANT.COM

The Green Tiger's Illustrated ABC

- Preface -

Uncountable thousands of alphabet books have been published. They were among the first books ever published for children, and the production of them continues unabated. The reasons for this are many. First, they are useful in teaching a child to read, for they make the abstract tangible; A is no longer, in their realm, a difficult concept, but is instead the governing letter of archer and apple and ape. With the addition of illustrations the letters come to life, and those of us who learned the alphabet in this way will always have a special fondness for antelopes, artichokes or whatever we met in that first adventure into letters. Second, alphabet books are appealing to publishers because most families with young children will need one or more ABC's. Third, they are popular with illustrators for they are an answer to the problem of how to use their skills and provide a marked path from the beginning to the end of the book. Further, since there is no author there is no need for the illustrator to share the royalties. Finally, alphabets are enjoyable for readers of all ages. The form of the letters, their familiar sequence and their relation to the real world is endlessly satisfying. It is a delight to see how each illustrator meets the challenges of each of the twenty-six letters.

In this book we at The Blue Lantern Studio have selected five favorite illustrations for each letter from our library of antique alphabet books. Artistic interest was our guiding principle. Another anthology could be made in which the selection was based on the rhymes which many ABC's utilize. We liked some illustrators' interpretations so much that we used them several times. It must not be imagined that this is any kind of historical survey of the alphabet book. The field is too vast, the examples overwhelming. Instead this is a collection of favorites that only hints at the richness and variety of the field, but we think it does the basic job of the alphabet book well—that is it makes many delightful connections between the letters of the alphabet and the world we live in. Following the A – Z section of The Green Tiger's Alphabet we offer a detailed bibliography and an illustrated essay on varying approaches to the making of an alphabet book.

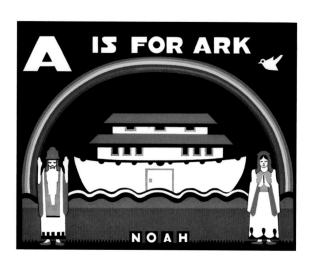

A IS FOR ARK

NOAH

Aa

A is an Airplane that flies in the sky; we stand on the ground and watch it sail by.

a

A stands for Adjutant Bird.

A for acrobats

B

Bear in despair

B IS FOR BULLDOG

B b

ball

B   BOAT   b

4

B for the Bunny, Furry and Cute

C is the Camel, well known in the East,
as a useful, a patient, and temperate beast.

Would you like to be a CLOUD Up in the sky alone?

C for cereal

C IS FOR COOKING; THE QUEEN THINKS IT FUN
TO MAKE TARTS FOR HER TEA, AND PUT JAM IN EACH ONE.
BUT THE KNAVE SEES THEM TOO, AND WHEN NO ONE IS LOOKING,
HE'LL SOON PUT AN END TO THE QUEEN OF HEARTS' COOKING.

CLOWN

Dd Dancing

D d	DEER	DUCK	DAD	DOG	DOLL
Dd					

**D was a Drummer
who played
with a grace.**

8

D for the DODO,
　no more we shall meet,
See his hooked bill,
　and his short wings and feet!

D

d is the
duck
with
floppity
feet

E e Eating

is the Elephant
whose trunk is his nose,
His arms, and his hands,
and his sprinkling hose.

E for eggs

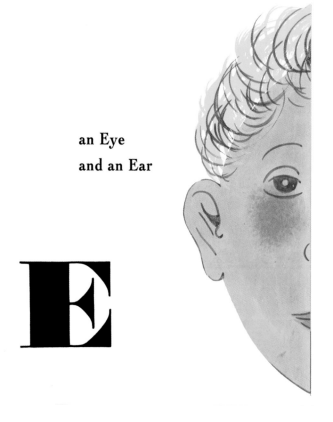

an Eye
and an Ear

Eyebright

F f

fruit

F f

F f

Fat French Frog's
Feel Fine and Free
Fingering the Fifes
You see.

F was the Fairy who
came through
the ceiling:
She said, "I've
dropped in just to
show my good feeling;
I like little Folk, and of Fun
I am Fond,
So you'll all come to life when
I waggle my wand."

12

G

**MASTER GOAT
AT HIS PORTRAIT
WILL SMILE**

Gg

G for girl

IS for Grizzly,
How wicked
he looks,
As he frightens the dollies,
And gnaws at the books!

gG

Giraffe

G is for Grapes
that are tasty
and sweet,
And for other things, too,
both to look at and eat.

H for
Happy Children

Hh Hopping

Hh for HORSE

HEY! diddle, diddle,
the cat and the fiddle,
The cow jumped
over the moon;

The little dog laughed to see such sport,
And the dish ran away with the spoon.

Iris

ink   Ice-cream

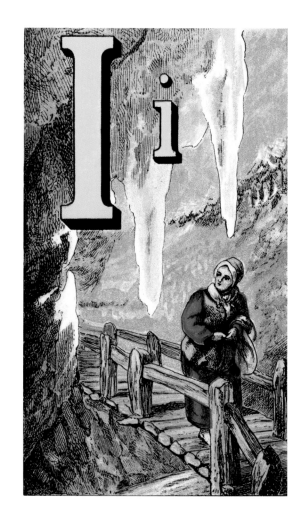

Here lies a very IDLE Pa,
Who slept beneath *his* umbrel*la*;
When, on waking, he found
That he'd slept the clock round;
So he shouted "Mum-Ma, Mum-Ma!"

I stands for **IBEX,** who borrowed a suit,
And set out to visit some cousins, on foot;
But they simply laughed at his comical "airs",
Till he fled from their nods and their whispers and stares.

J for Jackal, who sweeps the floors,
    And does a lot of other chores,
While the mermaids wash the dishes,
(These maids you know, are half
                    like fishes.)

J stands for the Jolly
    Good time, and the mirth
They all seem to have
    When they fly off the earth.

J j Jumping

Or would you be
a JACK-IN-THE-BOX
And scare just
everyone?

K

is for kiss ×××× Sally goes to ×× visit her aunt. Auntie kisses ×× her. Sally says, I came all alone.

k

 was once a little kite,
Kity,
　Whity,
　　Flighty,
　　　Kity,
Out of sighty, Little kite!

K was the King, and he popped out his head

Kk Kicking

KATIE'S kittens were so many,
Kipper, Kitty and Kilkenny,
Kevin, Kinky, Knutty, Kirsty.
She gave them milk when they
were thirsty.

L—longed for it

l letter

L

L Ladder.

L for the Lion, King of the Beasts

Ll Looking

MILK

M is for Mice
that picnic on crumbs,
(The two in the picture
are very good chums.)

Morning

matches

M for the Mermaids, so merry at play,
With bubbles for balls under rainbows of spray.

N n

Nightingales with Nimble Note
Nightly down the river float.

Nasturtium

Noah

N is for Naughtiness, found out you see.

N
n

N is a Nest in the
branch of a tree,
Where a family of
birds is as safe as can be.

O

open

O *is for*
OWEN'S

ORANGES
OAR
OVERALLS
OX

O o

O is for
oranges,
here there
are lots

Hurrah for old ocean,
So big and so grand!

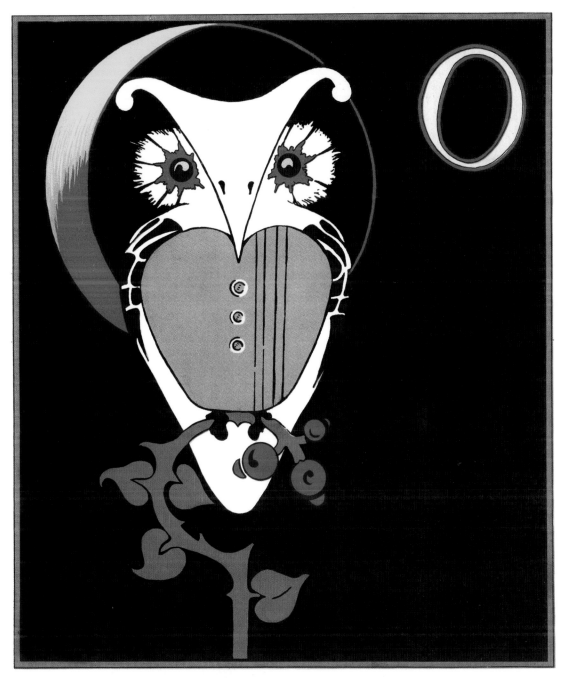

O o	OSTRICH	ONE	OWL	OIL	OARS
O o		1			

P for paints

P is a parrot
That says,
"Fine! Okay!"

P was once a little pump,
Pumpy,
Slumpy,
Flumpy,
Plumpy,
Dumpy, thumpy, Little pump!

P
stands for **PIG**,
who when bedtime came
round,
Made the whole sty with
his crying resound.
"Come here," said Mamma;
"you're not fit to be seen.
I'll show all the farm how
to make a Pig clean!"

Peacock

Qq Questioning

Quagga

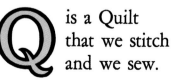

Q is a Quilt that we stitch and we sew.

"Quack! Quack!" says this duck.

Q

QUEEN Q

Running

Rod
Roger
River

Rat with a bat

R

r

robe

Sammy and Sally are soaked to the skin,
In a sharp summer storm they come scampering in.
Muddily splashing, all soggy and sopping,
Over the puddles they're jumping and hopping.

S is for
Strawberries

S is for Skates
to roll and to ride on.
Here is a smooth little
sidewalk to glide on.

Snow
Susie
Slide

S

T Toad on the road

T. t.

toys

T

U IS LIKE A BOWL

And U is not so hard to learn.
U stands for Uncle, Us, and Urn;
It's like a bowl, there is no doubt,
Where little goldfish swim about.

U begins umbrella to keep out the damp

undress

42

U Useful animal-our donkey Old Nell-
For years she has worked and has served us full well.

V for valentines

V is for Violet, a flower so sweet
Though nice to look at, not good to eat
How plain are the cabbages in their row
But cooked by Mummy are grand, you know!

V for Vicuna,
    who lives high
On peaks well up
    toward the sky.
Do you imagine
    that he knows
His wool is used
    to make fine clothes?

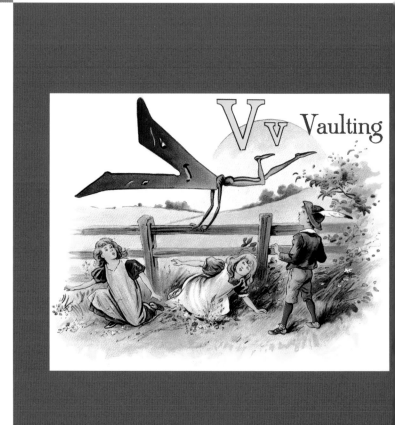

Vv Vaulting

V v U v	VASE	VINE	VAN	VISE	VEST

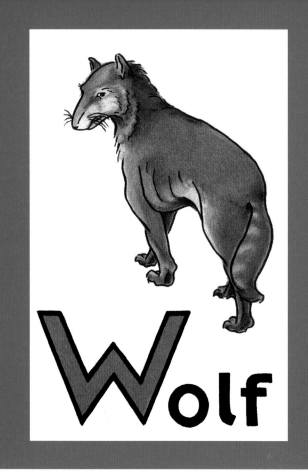

Wolf

Ww Winning

Ww is for Walrus,
a wonderful wag,
Who wears a white waist-coat
when punching the bag.

W

a Watermelon
on a Wagon
with a Wooden

W

WAGON
WALL
WOOD
WIGWAM
WHEEL
WATERING-
=CAN
WEATHER=
=VANE

Xylophone

X   X is for Xanadu

X·M·A·S SPELLS XMAS

X   X is the shape of the windmill's sails

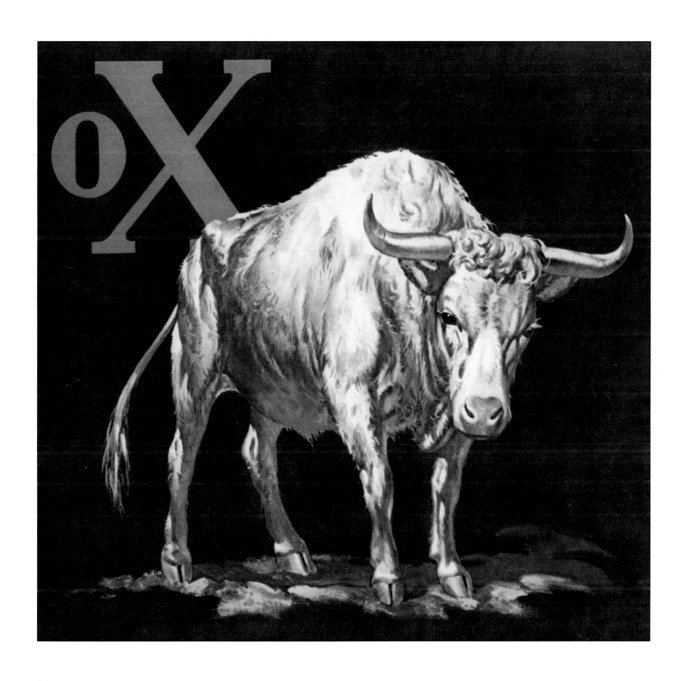

Y is for Youngsters, lively and gay,

—is for YAK, with hair long and fine,
Which Turks use for cloth that lasts for all time.

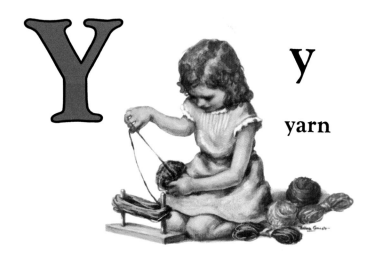

Y y

yarn

YACHT

 IS FOR YAWN

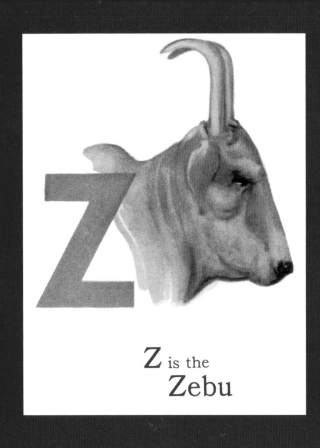

Z is the
Zebu

ZOO

Z for Zebra, with his hide
   Gayly striped all down the side.
He can travel with great speed,
But is very shy indeed.

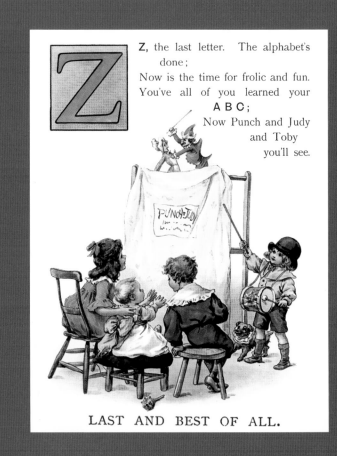

Z, the last letter. The alphabet's
   done;
Now is the time for frolic and fun.
You've all of you learned your
     A B C;
   Now Punch and Judy
     and Toby
      you'll see.

LAST AND BEST OF ALL.

Z for Zeppelin

ABC Picture Credits

Cover	Thelma Green. From *Alphabet Book,* 1939.
Endpapers	Unknown. *The ABC Book,* n.d.
Frontispiece	Maxfield Parrish. "Schooldays," 1908.
Title page	Unknown. From *Jolly Alphabets,* n.d.
Copyright	Unknown. From *The Comic Animal ABC,* n.d.
A • Page 2	(upper left) Carolyn S. Ashbrook. From *Our Alphabet of Toys,* 1932. (upper right) Unknown. From *Alphabet Poster Cards,* 1963. (lower left) Milo Winter. From *The Wonderful ABC Book,* 1946. (lower right) Harry B. Neilson. From *An Animal ABC,* c. 1920.
Page 3	Thelma Green. From *Alphabet Book,* 1939.
B • Page 4	(upper left) Fritz Eichenberg. From *Ape in a Cape,* 1952. (upper right) Clara Tice. From *ABC Dogs,* 1940. (lower left) Unknown. From *Alphabet Book,* 1939. (lower right) Robert Sallés. From *Je Saurai Lire,* n.d.
Page 5	Unknown. From *ABC Book,* 1925.
C • Page 6	(upper left) Unknown. From *An Alphabetical Arrangement of Animals for Little Naturalists,* 1821. (upper right) Florence Sarah Winship. From *ABC Picture Book,* 1948. (lower left) Thelma Green. From *Alphabet Book,* 1939. (lower right) E.W.B. From *The Wonder ABC Book,* c. 1950.
Page 7	Cicely Steed. From *The Wonder ABC Book,* c. 1950.
D • Page 8	(upper left) Alf. J. Johnson. From *ABC Land,* c. 1900. (upper right) Peter Mabie. From *The A to Z Book,* 1929. (lower left) Monro S. Orr. From *The Alphabet,* 1931. (lower right) Unknown. Illustration, n.d.
Page 9	Unknown. From *Tiny Tots' ABC,* n.d.
E • Page 10	(upper left) Alf. J. Johnson. From *ABC Land,* c. 1900. (upper right) W.W. Denslow. From *Denslow's One Ring Circus,* 1903. (lower left) Unknown. From *ABC Alphabet Book,* n.d. (lower right) Bruno Munari. From *Bruno Munari's ABC,* 1960.
Page 11	Cicely Mary Barker. From *A Flower Fairy Alphabet,* 1934.
F • Page 12	(upper left) Unknown. From *Alphabet Book,* 1939. (upper right) Milo Winter. From *Alphabet Book ABC,* 1938. (center) Unknown. From *The Comic Animal ABC,* n.d. (lower) Unknown. From *The Big ABC Book,* c. 1922.
Page 13	C.B. Falls. From *ABC Book,* 1923.
G • Page 14	(upper left) Harry B. Neilson. Illustration, n.d. (upper right) Unknown. From *ABC Alphabet Book,* n.d. (lower right) Unknown. From *Pour apprendre l'alphabet,* n.d. (lower left) Margaret Landers Sanford. From *The Teddy Bear ABC,* 1907.
Page 15	Stephen Stratton. From *An ABC Playbook,* 1945.
H • Page 16	(upper left) Michael Roberts. From *The Jungle ABC,* 1998. (upper right) Unknown. From *Toddler's ABC,* n.d. (lower left) Alf. J. Johnson. From *ABC Land,* c. 1900. (lower right) Garth Williams. From *The Big Golden Animal ABC,* 1954.
Page 17	Unknown. From *Mother Goose's ABC,* n.d.
I • Page 18	(upper left) Cicely Mary Barker. From *A Flower Fairy Alphabet,* 1934. (upper right) Unknown. (Japanese ABC,) n.d. (lower left) Ingles Rhode. From *The Gimcrack Jingle Alphabet,* c. 1900 (lower right) Unknown. From *Aunt Louisa's Alphabet Book,* n.d.
Page 19	Unknown. From *The Big ABC Book,* c. 1922.
J • Page 20	(upper left) Frederika Grosvenor. *The Noah's Ark ABC,* 1905. (upper right) Unknown. From *Our Air Ship ABC,* 1912. (lower left) Alf. J. Johnson. From *ABC Land,* c. 1900. (lower right) Florence Sarah Winship. From *ABC Picture Book,* 1948.
Page 21	Unknown. *Nursery Land ABC,* n.d.
K • Page 22	(upper) Françoise. From *The Gay ABC,* 1939. (upper center) Eulalie. From *The Bumper Book,* 1946. (lower center) Frank Adams. From *Arthur and the Boily Bird,* 1910. (lower) Alf. J. Johnson. From *ABC Land,* c. 1900.
Page 23	Janet and Anne Grahame - Johnstone. From *A Book of Children's Rhymes,* 1966.
L • Page 24	(upper right) Thelma Gooch. From *New Alphabet Book,* 1950. (lower right) Unknown. From *ABC Book,* 1925. (center left) Vojtêch Kubaˆsta. From *Sing A Song of Sixpence,* 1960. (lower left) Unknown. From *Aunt Louisa's Alphabet Book,* n.d.
Page 25	Alf. J. Johnson. From *ABC Land,* c. 1900.
M • Page 26	(upper left) Unknown. From *Easy Steps Picture Book,* 1945. (upper right) Milo Winter. From *Alphabet Book ABC,* 1938. (lower left) F.A. Brockhaus. From *Mein Erster Brockhaus,* 1970. (lower right) Unknown. From *My ABC Book,* n.d.
Page 27	Flora White. From *Peter Pan's ABC,* c. 1900.
N • Page 28	(upper left) Unknown. From *The Comic Animal ABC,* n.d. (upper right) Unknown. From *ABCD EFGH IJKLM,* 1943. (lower left) Unknown. From *The Child's Picture Book of Alphabets,* c. 1890. (lower right) Unknown. From *Pretty Picture ABC Book,* 1900.
Page 29	Milo Winter. From *Alphabet Book ABC,* 1938.
O • Page 30	(upper left) Helen Sewell. From *ABC For Every Day,* 1930. (upper right) Dorothy Buck. From *ABC of Names and Objects,* 1930. (lower left) Sep. E. Scott. From *Uncle Mac's Ladybird ABC Book,* 1950. (lower right) Bertha Corbett Melcher. From *The Sunbonnet Babies ABC Book,* 1929.
Page 31	Peter Mabie. From *The A to Z Book,* 1929.

ABC Picture Credits (cont.)

P • Page 32   (upper left) Unknown.
                   From *ABC*, 1949.
                   (upper right) Thelma Green.
                   From *Alphabet Book*, 1939.
                   (center) Eulalie.
                   From *The Bumper Book*, 1946.
                   (lower) Unknown.
                   From *The Big ABC Book*, c. 1922.

Page 33   Unknown. From *My ABC of Animals and Birds*, n.d.

Q • Page 34   (upper left) Alf. J. Johnson.
                   From *ABC Land*, c. 1900.
                   (upper right) Unknown.
                   From *The Child's Picture Book of Alphabets*, c. 1890.
                   (lower left) Racey Helps.
                   From *Happy Animals' ABC*, 1946.
                   (lower right) Unknown.
                   From *ABC of Games and Toys*, n.d.

Page 35   Cicely Steed.
                   From *The Wonder ABC Book*, c. 1950.

R • Page 36   (upper right) Alf. J. Johnson.
                   From *ABC Land*, c. 1900.
                   (upper left) Elsa Beskow.
                   From *ABC-resan*, 1960.
                   (lower left) Anne Anderson.
                   From *The Funny Bunny ABC*, 1912.
                   (lower right) Fritz Eichenberg.
                   From *Ape in a Cape*, 1952.

Page 37   Thelma Gooch.
                   From *New Alphabet Book*, 1950.

S • Page 38   (upper) Janet and Anne Grahame Johnstone.
                   From *A Book of Children's Rhymes*, 1966.
                   (center left) Unknown.
                   From *ABCD EFGH IJKLM*, 1943.
                   (center right) Milo Winter.
                   From *Alphabet Book ABC*, 1938.
                   (lower) Anne Anderson.
                   From *The Funny Bunny ABC*, 1912.

Page 39   Frances Brundage.
                   From *Boys and Girls from A to Z*, 1918.

T • Page 40   (upper left) Fritz Eichenberg.
                   From *Ape in a Cape*, 1952.
                   (upper right) Ottilia Adelborg.
                   From *Prinsarnes Blomsteralfabet*, 1930
                   (lower left) Corinne Ringel Bailey.
                   From *Alphabet Book*, 1934.
                   (lower right) Monica Beisner.
                   From *Folding Alphabet Book*, 1979.

Page 41   Sonia Delaunay. *Sonia Delaunay Alfabeto*, 1971.

U • Page 42   (upper left) D.E. Brahame.
                   From *My Very First Little Book of Letters*, n.d.
                   (upper right) Dorothy Chapman. From *ABC*, 1943.
                   (lower left) G.I. Smith.
                   From *Tiny Tots' ABC*, n.d.
                   (lower right) Helen Sewell.
                   From *ABC For Every Day*, 1930

Page 43   A.E. Kennedy. From *Feather and Fur ABC*, 1911.

V • Page 44   (upper left) Selma Gooch.
                   From *Alphabet Book*, 1939.
                   (upper right) Unknown.
                   From *Baby's Own All Colour Picture Annual*, 1954.
                   (lower left) Frederika Grosvenor.
                   The Noah's Ark ABC, 1905.
                   (lower right) Alf. J. Johnson. From *ABC Land*, c. 1900

Page 45   Peter Mabie. From *The A to Z Book*, 1929.

W • Page 46   (upper left) Hete Köppen. *Tier-Alphabet*, c. 1920
                   (upper right) Alf. J. Johnson. From *ABC Land*, c. 1900.
                   (lower left) W.W. Denslow.
                   From *Denslow's One Ring Circus*, 1903.
                   (lower right) Bruno Munari. From *Bruno Munari's ABC*, 1960.

Page 47   Unknown. From *ABC of Objects & Number Book*, 1932.

X • Page 48   (upper left) Blanchard. From *Bibiche et son alphabet*, 1948.
                   (upper right) Hendrik Willem Van Loon.
                   From *Around The World With The Alphabet*, 1935.
                   (lower left) Unknown. *The ABC Book*, n.d.
                   (lower right) G.I. Smith. From *Tiny Tots' ABC*, n.d.

Page 49   Unknown. From *My ABC of Animals and Birds*, n.d.

Y • Page 50   (upper left) Unknown.
                   From *Pretty Picture ABC Book*, 1900.
                   (upper right) Constance White.
                   From *Animal ABC Book*, 1910.
                   (lower left) Thelma Gooch.
                   From *New Alphabet Book*, 1950.
                   (lower right) Unknown.
                   From *Easy Steps Picture Book*, 1945.

Page 51   Clare Turlay Newberry. From *The Kittens' ABC*, 1965.

Z • Page 52   (upper left) Unknown. From *ABCD EFGH IJKLM*, 1943.
                   (upper right) Corinne Ringel Bailey.
                   From *Alphabet Book*, 1934.
                   (lower left) Frederika Grosvenor. *The Noah's Ark ABC*, 1905.
                   (lower right) Unknown. From *ABC of Games and Toys*, n.d.

Page 53   Unknown. From *ABC Alphabet Book*, n.d.

Approaches to the Alphabet Book

Page 56   (upper left) Leonard Everett Fisher.
                   From *The ABC Exhibit*, 1991.
                   (upper right) Bryan Ward. From *Ant and Bee*, n.d.
                   (lower left) David Pelletier. From *The Graphic Alphabet*, 1996.
                   (lower right) Grace G. Drayton. From *A Spartan Primer*, 1913.

Page 57   (upper left) Chris Van Allsburg. From *Z was Zapped*, 1987.
                   (upper right) Johnny Gruelle.
                   From *Raggedy Ann's Alphabet Book*, 1925.
                   (lower left) Wanda Gág. From *The ABC Bunny*, 1933.
                   (lower right) Frances Brundage. From *Mother Goose ABC*, 1913.

Page 58   (upper) Kate Greenaway. From *A Apple Pie*, 1886.
                   (lower) Seymour Chwast. From *The Alphabet Parade*, 1991.

Page 59   (upper left) Eileen Mayo. From *Nature's ABC*, n.d.
                   (upper right) Unknown.
                   From *Good Times with ABC*, 1946.
                   (lower left) Pauline Batchelder Adams.
                   From *The Jingling ABC's*, 1929.
                   (lower right) Unknown. From *ABC Painting Book*, 1960.

Page 60   (upper left) Kathleen Lucas. From *In Flowerland ABC*, n.d.
                   (upper right) Tony Palazzo.
                   From *An Elephant Alphabet*, 1961.
                   (lower left) Unknown. From *Off by Train ABC*, n.d.
                   (lower right) Unknown. From *Puppy Dog's ABC*, c. 1900.

Page 61   (upper left and lower right) Sybil Rebman.
                   From *Animal Alphabet*, 1917.
                   (upper right and lower left) Roberto de Vicq de Cumptich.
                   From *Bembo's Zoo: An Animal ABC Book*, 2000.

Page 62   (upper left) Italo Lupi. *Found alphabet*, n.d.
                   (upper right) Stephen T. Johnson.
                   From *Alphabet City*, 1995.
                   (lower left and lower right) Phil May. From *Phil May's ABC*, 1897.

Back Cover   Thelma Green. From *Alphabet Book*, 1939.

Yo - y o

▼ ▼ ▼

NOUNS

As you will see from a perusal of this volume, nouns are the over-whelming favorite of ABC makers. The obvious reason is that nouns are things, and the pictur-ing of things is simple and straightforward. As

almost all alphabet books are designed to instruct the young child, the simplicity of nouns provides a con-crete and satisfying beginning for the future reader.

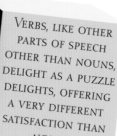

VERBS

VERBS ARE RARELY USED AS THE ORGANIZING IDEA FOR AN ABC. THEY DO NOT OFFER THE SECURITY OF IDENTIFICATION THAT NOUNS DO. EVEN THOUGH GRACE DRAYTON OFFERS US THREE EXAMPLES, IT TAKES SOME THOUGHT TO SEE WHAT SHE IS ILLUSTRATING.

VERBS, LIKE OTHER PARTS OF SPEECH OTHER THAN NOUNS, DELIGHT AS A PUZZLE DELIGHTS, OFFERING A VERY DIFFERENT SATISFACTION THAN NOUNS.

Rip

ADJECTIVES

ADJECTIVES ARE EVEN MORE BAFFLING THAN VERBS. IT IS NOT CLEAR, UNTIL VAN ALLSBURG TELLS US, THAT THE L IS TOO LARGE, NOR IS IT APPARENT THAT PRETTINESS IS THE SUBJECT OF THE CHILD HOLDING THE MASK. AGAIN, HOWEVER, CHALLENGE OFFERS DELIGHT.

The L was much too

P is for Pretty, you never can hide
Your prettiness if you are sunny inside.

OTHER PARTS OF SPEECH

THERE ARE SO MANY ABC'S THAT ONE COULD, WITH MUCH SEARCHING, MAKE A COLLECTION OF EXAMPLES BASED ON VARIOUS PARTS OF SPEECH. THE RABBIT AND THE WANDERING YOUTH ARE DEMONSTRATING ADVERBS.

A   As I was going up Pippen Hill,—
       Pippen Hill was dirty,—
       There I met a pretty Miss,
       And she dropped me a curtsey.

U

for Up and Up-side-down

OPENED IT

A STORY TOLD

THE COMMONEST THEME FOR A STORYTELLING ALPHABET IS "A APPLE PIE." IT TELLS ALL OF THE ADVENTURES OF AN APPLE PIE ENCOUNTERING HUNGRY HUMANS.

KATE GREENAWAY'S VERSION (SHOWN HERE) IS THE BEST-KNOWN VERSION, BUT SHE DID NOT INVENT THE CONCEPT. IT IS AN ANONYMOUS CREATION, PROBABLY FROM THE 18TH CENTURY.

P PEEPED IN IT

AN EVENT

SEYMOUR CHWAST'S ALPHABET PARADE IS ONE OF THE BEST-REALIZED EXAMPLES OF AN ABC THAT USES AN EVENT OR SITUATION AS THE STRUCTURE OF A BOOK.

IT IS WONDERFUL HOW HE SHOWS US THINGS BEGINNING WITH EACH LETTER, AND INCORPORATES THE LETTER ITSELF INTO THE PARADE — AS THE LADDER FORMING THE A ON WHICH ACROBATS AND AN ACCORDIONIST PERFORM.

J j Jackdaws & Jays belong to the bird family called 'crows'. They can copy the sounds made by other animals. The jay mimics other birds & the voices of cats, lambs & pigs: the jackdaw can be taught to speak.

E is for Eskimo, with line and hook,
F is for Fish, which his mother will cook.

RELATED OBJECTS

IT IS EASY TO JUST THROW OBJECTS TOGETHER THAT ALL BEGIN WITH THE SAME LETTER, BUT A LITTLE MORE DIFFICULT TO FIND A RELATION BETWEEN THEM. THE TWO J BIRDS ARE ONE KIND OF RELATION, THE ESKIMO AND THE FISH QUITE ANOTHER.

C cat
clock
chair

Nick and Nock went nutling

THEMATIC ABC'S

Alphabet books, in which each letter is chosen out of the vocabulary of a single subject, are very common. Early in the history of children's books bible alphabets abounded. Other popular themes are: history, occupations, children's names, toys, geography, domestic animals, wild animals, nursery rhymes, foreign lands, and botany.

Lion

L for the Lion –
How loud he can roar!
If we made such a noise
Our throats would be sore!

PICTURES MADE FROM THE LETTERS

HERE ARE TWO APPROACHES TO THE CHALLENGE OF DEPICTING AN ANIMAL OUT OF THE LETTERS WITH WHICH ITS NAME IS SPELLED. SYBIL REBMAN USES CALLIGRAPHY TO WONDERFULLY WRITE-OUT THE NAME OF EACH ANIMAL.

ROBERTO DE VICQ DE CUMPTICH ALSO TAKES THE APPROACH OF USING THE LETTERS CONTAINED IN THE ANIMAL'S NAME TO CONSTRUCT THE IMAGE. HE LIMITS HIMSELF BY USING RIGID TYPE FORMS, BUT MAKES THE TASK POSSIBLE BY ABANDONING SEQUENCE, AND USING THE LETTERS MANY TIMES.

Quail

Q for the Quail,
In the Autumn they fly –
And taste very good
When made into pie!

FOUND LETTERS

THIS MINOR, BUT ENTERTAINING CATEGORY INVOLVES SEARCING THE WORLD FOR NATURALLY OCCURRING LETTERFORMS. THE STOPLIGHT IS ONE OF TWENTY-SIX STRIKING PHOTOGRAPHS OF THINGS FOUND IN EVERYDAY LIFE. THE STONES, WITH THEIR NATURALLY OCCURRING LETTERS, WERE FOUND BY ITALO LUPI ON THE BEACH. FOR THE FUTURE READER.

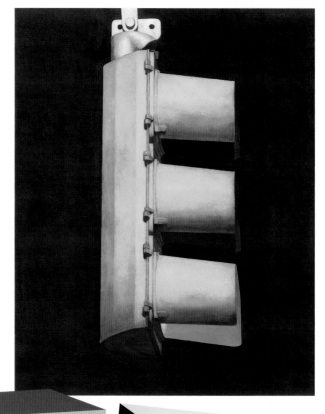

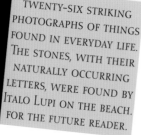

THE ALPHABET AS A PUZZLE

ANY ABC WHICH DEPICTS A PICTURE AND A LETTER WITOUT EXPLANATION AS TO THEIR CONNECTION IS, TO SOME EXTENT, A PUZZLE. YOUNG CHILDREN MAY TAKE A LITTLE TIME TO COMPREHEND THAT THE PICTURED OBJECT IS BREAD, WHICH STARTS WITH B. OLDER READERS ARE LARGELY UNFAZED WITH CHALLENGES OF THIS SORT, BUT A FEW ARTISTS ENJOY BEING OBSCURE. I HAVE FOUND NO ALPHABET AS DIFFICULT AS PHIL MAYS'. I HAVE REVIEWED IT MANY TIMES, AND CAN ONLY MAKE A REASONABLE GUESS ABOUT HALF THE TIME. MORE BAFFLING STILL IS HIS KEY TO SOLUTION THAT PROVIDES NOTHING BUT A DEEPER MYSTERY.

COLOPHON

Book & cover design by
Chev Darling & Moses Gershbein
at Blue Lantern Studio

Typeset in Diotima & Futura

Printed by
Star Standard Industries

A—APPLE · PIE

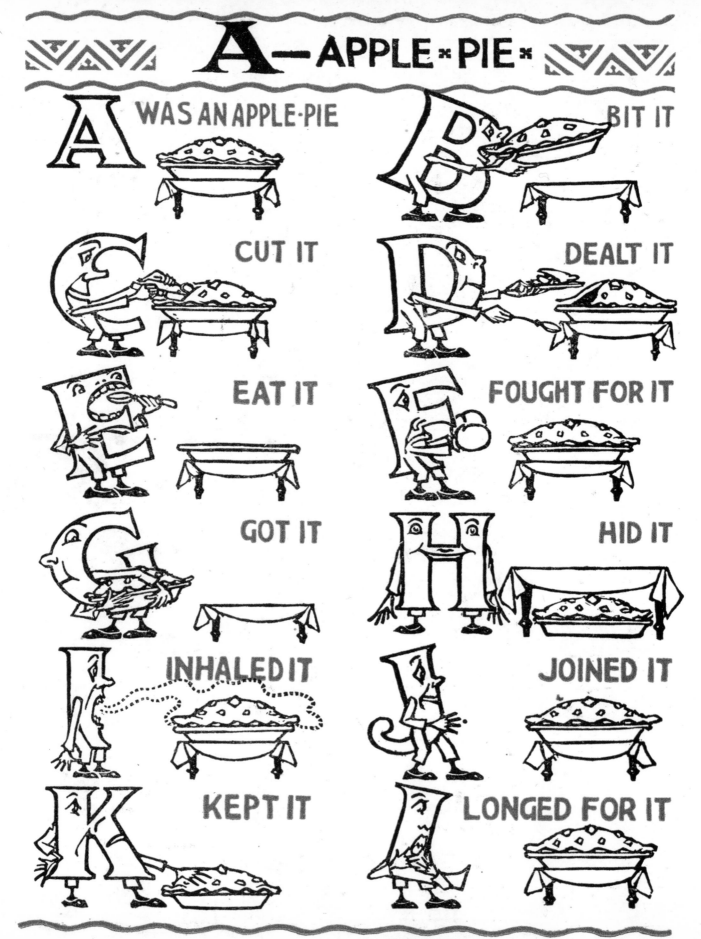

A WAS AN APPLE-PIE

B BIT IT

C CUT IT

D DEALT IT

E EAT IT

F FOUGHT FOR IT

G GOT IT

H HID IT

I INHALED IT

J JOINED IT

K KEPT IT

L LONGED FOR IT